# What Do We Know About the Curse of King Tut's Tomb?

by Ben Hubbard

illustrated by Manuel Gutierrez

Penguin Workshop

To Paula Manzanero, with thanks—BH

For you, future Egyptologist—MG

PENGUIN WORKSHOP
An imprint of Penguin Random House LLC
1745 Broadway, New York, New York 10019

First published in the United States of America by Penguin Workshop,
an imprint of Penguin Random House LLC, 2025

Copyright © 2025 by Penguin Random House LLC

Penguin Random House values and supports copyright. Copyright fuels creativity,
encourages diverse voices, promotes free speech, and creates a vibrant culture. Thank you
for buying an authorized edition of this book and for complying with copyright laws by
not reproducing, scanning, or distributing any part of it in any form without permission.
You are supporting writers and allowing Penguin Random House to continue to publish
books for every reader. Please note that no part of this book may be used or reproduced in
any manner for the purpose of training artificial intelligence technologies or systems.

PENGUIN is a registered trademark and PENGUIN WORKSHOP is a trademark
of Penguin Books Ltd. WHO HQ & Design is a registered trademark
of Penguin Random House LLC.

Visit us online at penguinrandomhouse.com.

Library of Congress Cataloging-in-Publication Data is available.

Printed in the United States of America

ISBN 9780593888575 (paperback)          10 9 8 7 6 5 4 3 2 1 CJKW
ISBN 9780593888582 (library binding)     10 9 8 7 6 5 4 3 2 1 CJKW

The authorized representative in the EU for product safety and compliance is
Penguin Random House Ireland, Morrison Chambers, 32 Nassau Street,
Dublin D02 YH68, Ireland, https://eu-contact.penguin.ie.

# Contents

# What Do We Know About the Curse of King Tut's Tomb?

On November 26, 1922, Howard Carter walked down a long, dark corridor leading underground into the sands of the Egyptian desert. At the end was a door to a tomb that had been closed for over three thousand years.

The door was stamped with the name of an ancient Egyptian pharaoh (king), Tutankhamun (say: toot-an-KHA-moon).

Carter was an archaeologist, someone who studies ancient cultures by unearthing the objects created by them. He had been digging for years in his search for Tutankhamun's tomb. At last, he had found it. His hands trembled as he held a candle up to the door.

Carter was not alone. Standing behind him was Englishman Lord Carnarvon and his daughter, Evelyn. Carnarvon was a wealthy aristocrat who had paid for Carter's expedition and work to find the tomb. Like Carter, Carnarvon was fascinated by ancient Egypt. Now it seemed they were about to make a great discovery. Carter picked up an iron rod and poked a hole through the top left-hand corner of the plaster door. He put his candle through the hole to see what was inside. The hot, musty air that escaped made the candle flicker.

Slowly, Carter's eyes adjusted to the light and he could see strange shapes among the shadows. There were statues, furniture, and the glint of gold everywhere.

Carter stood still, dumbstruck. The treasures in the tomb were beyond his wildest imagination.

"Can you see anything?" Carnarvon asked anxiously. "Yes," Carter finally managed to reply. "Wonderful things."

It was an extraordinary moment. Although many archaeologists knew the name "Tutankhamun," few believed his tomb would ever be discovered.

No one expected it would be found with its treasures intact. Many pharaohs were laid to rest with a large amount of precious objects, and their tombs were often plundered by robbers, some soon after the pharaoh had been buried.

In ancient Egypt, entering the tomb of the pharaoh and stealing from it was a serious crime. Those who were caught would be executed. And it was believed that those who were not caught might be struck down by a curse. A pharaoh's curse was like a spell, a punishment that was said to bring bad luck, illness, or even death. Specific curses were sometimes written near the entrance of a pharaoh's tomb to warn intruders and thieves away.

Howard Carter had not seen a curse posted at Tutankhamun's tomb. But nothing would stop him from entering even if he had. Discovering the tomb and all its contents was an archaeologist's dream. Carter did not know it yet, but he had just made the largest discovery of Egyptian treasures in history. But perhaps he was also about to uncover something disturbing and frightening.

Because soon after discovering the tomb, strange things began to happen to those involved. These events led many to believe that the pharaoh himself was punishing those who had disturbed his resting place from beyond the grave. In finding the pharaoh's tomb, had Carter also unleashed the curse of Tutankhamun on the world?

# CHAPTER 1
## The Boy King

Tutankhamun is often called "the boy king." That's because he was only eight years old when he became pharaoh, in 1333 BCE. Although he was young, Tutankhamun had inherited one of the most advanced civilizations of the ancient world.

Even at that time, Egyptians were already expert builders and engineers, highly skilled scientists and scholars, and accomplished artists and craftspeople. In addition to their pyramids, temples, and palaces, Egyptians had created a written language and complex religion, and made beautiful jewelry, sculptures, and wall paintings.

Egypt's pharaoh was like a living god on Earth. Almost always male, the pharaoh was believed to be unbeatable on the battlefield and wore a crown with a uraeus (say: YOO-ree-uhs), a small cobra figure that could supposedly spit fire at his enemies. The cobra was also the symbol for the goddess Wadjet (say: WAAD-jet), one of the many gods the Egyptian people worshipped.

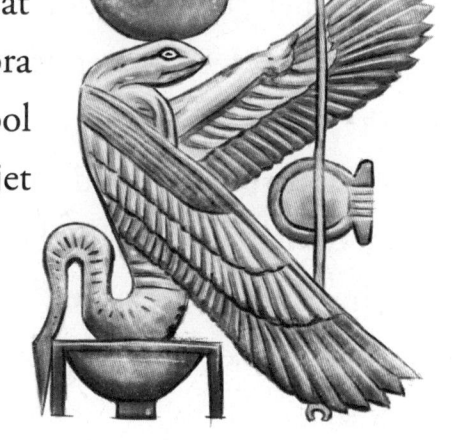

The goddess Wadjet

The Egyptian gods also included Amon-Re (say: AH-muhn-ray), the king of the gods, and Osiris (say: OH-sai-rus), the god of the afterlife. In Egyptian wall paintings, Osiris is often shown alongside Anubis (say: uh-NOO-bis), the god of mummification. The Egyptians believed that after death, a person would be judged by Anubis, who would then weigh the person's heart against a feather to see if they were without sin. If the heart was as light as the feather, the person would be presented to Osiris and allowed to enter the afterlife. If the heart was heavier than the feather, it was gobbled up and the dead person would no longer exist.

Preparing for death was extremely important to the Egyptians. And the Egyptian pharaohs were buried with everything they would need in the afterlife: clothes, food, furniture, and personal possessions. A pharaoh's tomb was filled with treasures and decorated with painted murals.

Anubis and the weighing of the heart ceremony

It often took years to prepare the tomb and the interior space. For example, Pharaoh Khufu began designing his tomb as soon as he inherited the throne, in around 2550 BCE. This took around twenty years to complete and it became one of the largest stone structures ever constructed: the Great Pyramid at Giza.

A pharaoh could not be disturbed after being buried in his tomb. Those who broke this rule were in danger of being cursed. Curses were

written at the entrance of tombs, or sometimes inside the tomb on a stone tablet. One example read: "Cursed be those who disturb the rest of a Pharaoh. They that shall break the seal of this tomb shall meet death by disease that no doctor can diagnose."

A curse on another tomb read: "All people who enter this tomb who will make evil against this tomb and destroy it: may the crocodile be against them in water, and snakes against them on land. May the hippopotamus be against them in water, the scorpion on land." This meant the curse for entering and damaging the tomb would be attacks by crocodiles, snakes, hippopotamuses, and scorpions. The curse would find you wherever you were: on land or in the water.

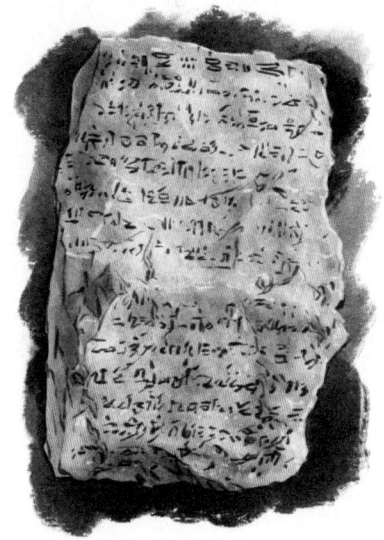

# Ancient Egypt

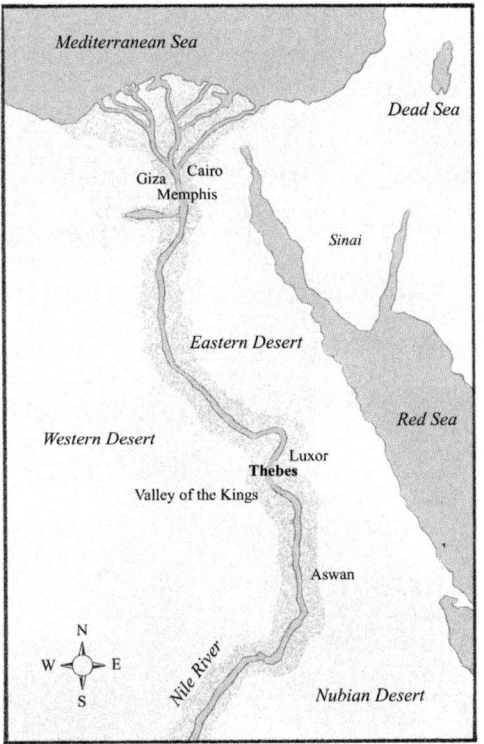

Located in hot, dry North Africa, Egyptian culture began around 6000 BCE as groups of small farms along the Nile River. Every year, the

Nile flooded the farmland, bringing rich soil and nutrients carried by the water onto the land. This made Egypt a fertile place with plenty of food.

Over thousands of years, Egypt grew into a wealthy kingdom ruled over by powerful kings, called pharaohs. The pharaohs constructed cities, such as Thebes, Aswan, Luxor, and Memphis (near today's capital, Cairo), and massive pyramids near Giza to be buried in. Later pharaohs built their tombs underground in the Valley of the Kings.

These warnings were supposed to scare intruders and robbers away. But the Egyptians realized the curses were not enough to keep tombs safe. Hundreds of years later, it was decided to bury the pharaohs in underground tombs in a secret location. This location became known as the Valley of the Kings.

The Valley of the Kings is a dry, lifeless place located in the Theban Mountains. Here, temperatures can reach 120 degrees and there is a blinding glare from the dazzling white limestone rock. Normally there would be little reason to go to the Valley of the Kings. This is exactly why it was chosen to bury Egypt's pharaohs, between 1539 and 1075 BCE. Unlike the Giza location, tombs in the Valley of the Kings were not marked by giant pyramids. The valley was a barren area where underground tombs could be concealed—a place where kings and queens could rest in peace for eternity. One such tomb would belong to Tutankhamun.

Unlike Pharaoh Khufu, Tutankhamun did not start planning his tomb right away. He was a young boy who depended on advisers to help him rule. As a young boy and teenager, Tutankhamun had a pleasurable life in luxurious palaces. Servants attended to his every need: bathing and dressing him and bringing him food. He spent time hunting in his chariot with a bow and arrows or taking boat trips down the Nile.

He dressed in fine white cotton and jewelry made of gold and precious stones. He wanted for nothing.

However, Tutankhamun had inherited a troubled kingdom. His father had been the unpopular ruler Amenhotep (say: AH-muhn-how-tep) IV. Amenhotep had announced that Egypt would only worship one god, Aten the sun god, and closed most of the country's temples. He then changed his name to Akhenaten (say: AH-kuh-naa-tin)

Aten the sun god

and built a new capital city in the middle of the desert. Suddenly, all the other gods people had worshipped their whole lives were gone, and thousands of priests who had been dedicated to each specific god were unemployed. Akhenaten was so disliked that people destroyed his statues after he died.

Akhenaten

Egyptians were relieved when the new pharaoh, Tutankhamun, restored the old religious system. He became a well-liked ruler who, at age ten, married his sister, the thirteen-year-old princess Ankhesenamun (say: ANK-KESS-in-i-min). This was not considered unusual at the time.

Marrying within the family helped ensure the line of succession, and the family would continue to rule without being challenged. The couple were fond of each other, but their marriage did not last. At eighteen years old, Tutankhamun died suddenly. Some think he was murdered, perhaps by a blow to the head by one of his own advisers. Few people had expected Tutankhamun's death.

His tomb had not yet been prepared. But his burial had to take place quickly so his journey to the afterlife could begin.

Before being buried, a pharaoh had to be mummified. This was a process of preserving the body. The organs such as the lungs, liver, and stomach were removed and placed in special

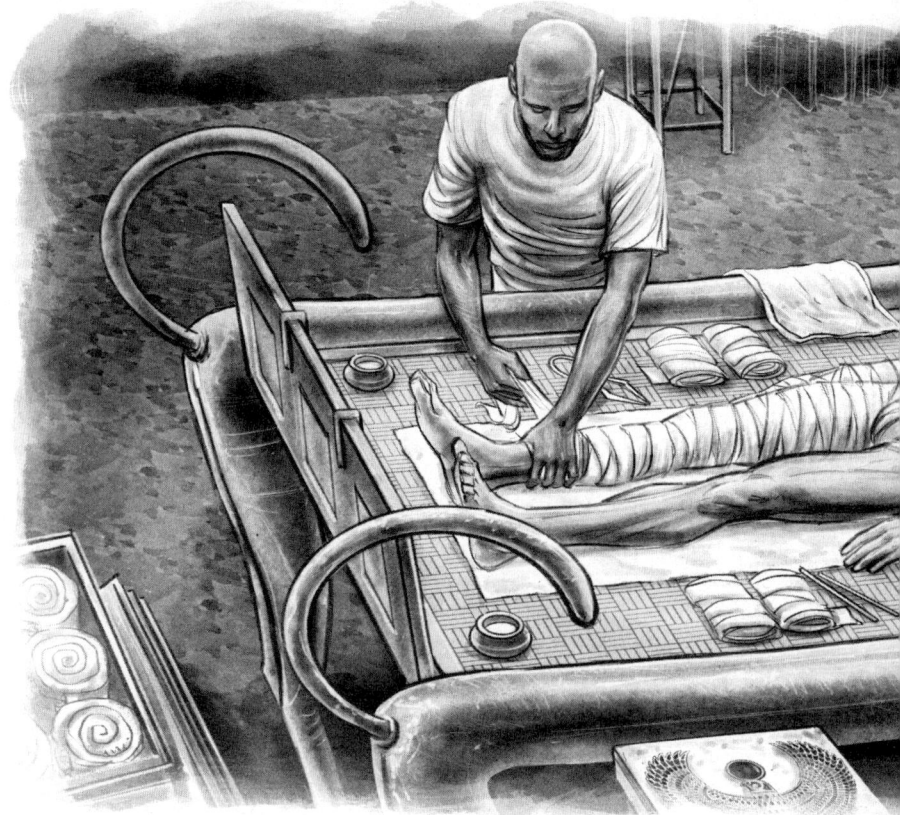

jars. A hook was pushed into the nostrils and used to pull out the brain. The body was then covered in salt and stuffed with straw to dry it out. This was the ancient Egyptian style of embalming. After forty days, the stuffing was taken out and replaced with linen. Finally, Tutankhamun's body was wrapped in strips of linen and placed in a coffin.

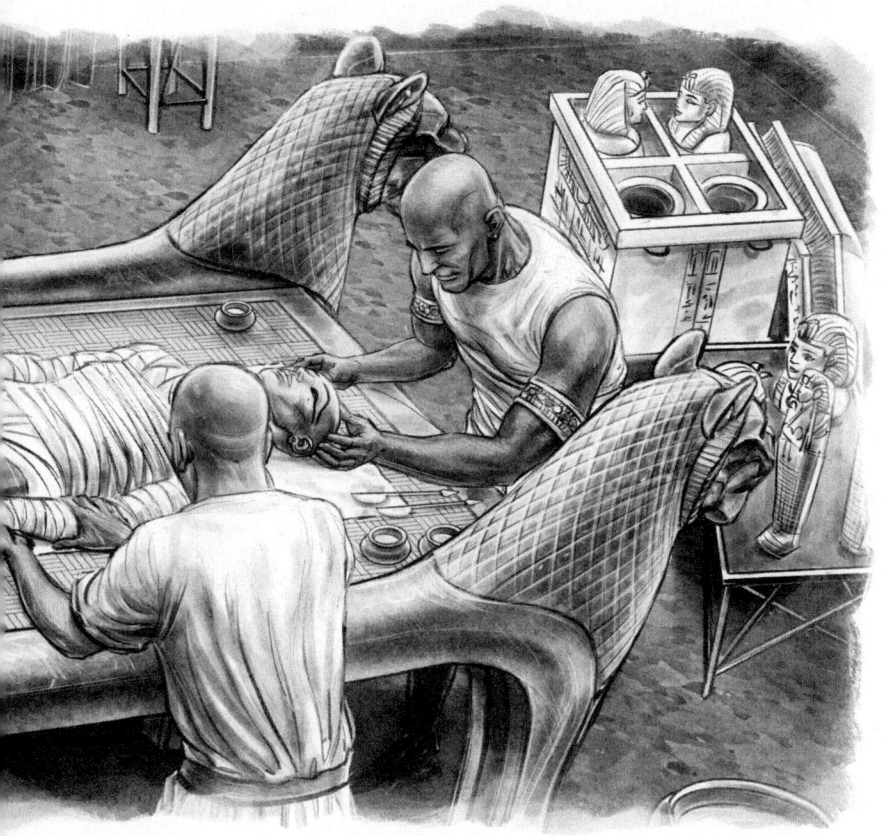

It was not only humans who were mummified in Egypt—animals were, too, including cats, birds, crocodiles, and even fish. Some pharaohs were buried with their mummified pets. However, the most care was given to the bodies of the pharaohs.

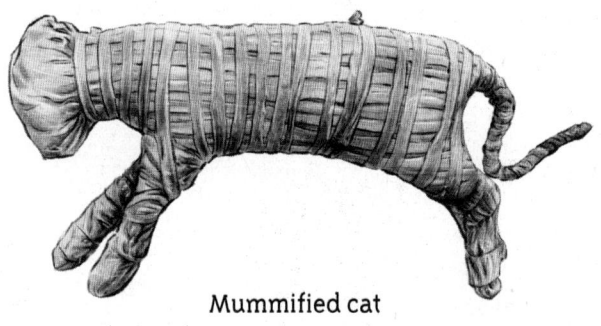

Mummified cat

After mummification, Tutankhamun was carried to his tomb in the Valley of the Kings during a secret ceremony. No one besides those involved in the burial could know where his body was placed. As his servants and priests left the tomb, they sealed up the doors with plaster. Tutankhamun and his possessions would lie undisturbed for thousands of years.

# CHAPTER 2
## Raiding Egypt

As the bodies of the Egyptian pharaohs lay in their underground tombs, the world above changed. Over time, other cultures invaded Egypt, including the Romans and the Ottoman Empire. The once great civilization of Egypt faded. By the modern age, little of ancient Egypt remained, except its huge stone pyramids and temples. But few people were interested in these ancient buildings or the culture that constructed them.

This changed in 1798, when French general Napoleon Bonaparte invaded Egypt, more than three thousand years after the time of the pharaohs. With Napoleon were scientists who were amazed by the ancient wonders they found there. They created the Egyptian Scientific Institute to show what they had discovered to the world beyond Egypt.

Napoleon invades Egypt, 1798

When the Institute scientists entered the Valley of the Kings, they found eleven pharaoh tombs that had been opened. The tombs had been robbed of their artifacts—all the objects left behind by an ancient culture. The scientists set about making a map of the valley and found a hole in a cliff wall. With candles in hand, they crept through the hole and stood in the almost empty tomb. The walls were covered with colorfully painted murals and some small wooden statues were scattered on the ground. They did not know it at the time, but this was the tomb of Amenhotep III, Tutankhamun's grandfather.

East wall of Amenhotep III's tomb

The French scientists packaged up the statues with other objects they found in Egypt, including jewelry, pottery, and furniture. They published an account of their findings in a book called *Description of Egypt*. The book and the Egyptian artifacts caused a great stir in Europe and the United States—a trend called "Egyptomania." Beginning in the early nineteenth century, treasure hunters started traveling to

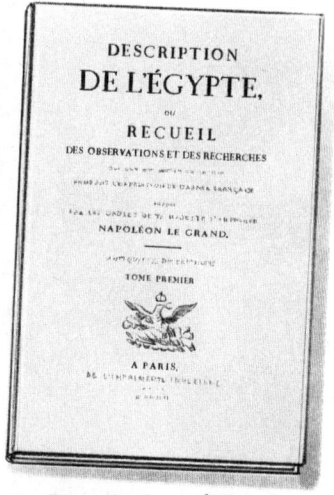

*Description of Egypt*

Egypt to buy and steal any artifacts they could find. These could be sold for large prices back at home.

Some of the artifacts the treasure hunters discovered beginning in the 1800s were mummies. These were not only found in tombs but also in shops and street markets. Some local Egyptians, eager to make money, helped the foreigners obtain them. The mummies were then shipped back to Europe and the United States as souvenirs.

# Ancient Tomb Robbers

Tomb robbing, or looting, has a long history in Egypt. It became especially common during the time the pyramids at Giza were built. Then, royal tombs built inside the pyramids were piled high with objects containing silver, gold, and semiprecious stones.

To stop or confuse thieves, the pyramids were built with false doors and secret passageways. But the robbers almost always found a way in. Even after pharaohs moved their burial site to the Valley of the Kings, their tombs were still plundered. The punishment for tomb robbing in ancient Egypt was execution with a wooden stake.

Some mummies were unwrapped before a crowd, at universities, hospitals, and private homes. At "mummy unwrapping parties," a mummy would have its linen wrappings removed by the host to entertain the guests. Some hoped to find treasure wound up in the folds of the cloth.

# Giovanni Belzoni (1778–1823)

One of the first modern treasure hunters to raid Egypt was Italian Giovanni Belzoni. Belzoni was not a scientist but a circus performer determined to get rich from Egyptian treasure. Nothing was too big for Belzoni to steal. In 1817,

Giovanni Belzoni

he discovered the tomb of Pharaoh Seti I in the Valley of the Kings. Ancient tomb robbers had already taken everything except for Seti's beautifully carved white sarcophagus. Although it was made of solid alabaster stone, Belzoni hauled the massive sarcophagus from the tomb and onto a boat on the Nile. From there, it was shipped to Sir John Soane's Museum in London, England, where it remains today.

The ancient Egyptians believed that amulets—small pieces of jewelry or charms—could protect the dead during their journey to the afterlife. And so these tiny treasures were sometimes wrapped into the folds of the embalming cloth. But the body beneath the cloth would be even more amazing. The ancient Egyptians were so good at embalming, the flesh and skin were usually completely intact. Guests at a mummy unwrapping party often found themselves gazing at the face of someone who had lived over three thousand years earlier.

To Europeans and Americans, Egypt was a strange, magical place. They wondered if the ancient Egyptians knew special secrets about life after death.

Mummies became so popular that they started appearing in stories and novels. In 1827, nearly thirty years after Napoleon had invaded Egypt, English author Jane C. Loudon published

*The Mummy!* The book is about a pharaoh, named Khufu, who comes back to life in the future, the year 2126 to be exact. This pharaoh looks like a monster, but instead of attacking people, he offers

advice about life and politics. However, not all fictional mummies were as friendly. (Khufu was the pharaoh who had built the Great Pyramid at Giza around 2550 BCE, but this book was not really about him.)

In 1869, American author Louisa May Alcott published "Lost in a Pyramid, or the Mummy's Curse." In this horror story, two explorers break into Khufu's Great Pyramid at Giza. Inside, they discover a mummy and a curse written on a piece of parchment (a type of paper made from the skin of an animal).

The curse promises harm to anyone who disturbs the mummy's grave. After returning home, both men suffer misfortune and tragedy. It was the first time that a curse and a mummy were mentioned in a popular story. The idea would stick in the public's mind.

By the end of the nineteenth century, the engineering marvels and powerfully built wonders of Egypt were attracting a new wave of visitors. These people were not only treasure hunters but also archaeologists fascinated by ancient Egyptian culture. Howard Carter was among them.

# CHAPTER 3
## Carter and Carnarvon

Howard Carter was a seventeen-year-old artist when he fell in love with ancient Egypt. His job at that time was creating drawings of real Egyptian artifacts at a family estate in England. Carter illustrated jewelry, coffins, and statues of gods and goddesses. Then in 1891, he got a chance to travel to Cairo and draw some recently discovered Egyptian tombs. He was soon on a boat to North Africa.

Carter worked hard at his new job. He started early, finished late, and lived in a simple home. But he loved it. Drawing the inside of tombs and their brightly painted walls fascinated Carter. Before long he had learned to decode the ancient Egyptian writing known as hieroglyphics. Made up of picture symbols, hieroglyphs were often written on tomb walls. Carter became well-respected and was soon helping archaeologist Flinders Petrie excavate (dig up) artifacts. Petrie was known as "the father of archaeology." He showed Carter how to dig for objects carefully, using brushes and small instruments. He also taught him how to search for tombs.

Flinders Petrie

Before long, Carter had become a full-time archaeologist, digging for ancient Egyptian artifacts in the hot sun. Archaeologists in Egypt had to schedule their digs between late fall and early spring. It was too hot to work at any other time. Carter would dig alongside a crew of Egyptian workers, sifting through sand and rummaging through rubble. Six years later, officials at the Egyptian Antiquities Service offered him the job of chief inspector in Egypt. This put him in charge of excavating Saqqara (say: suh-KAA-ruh), the burial site for the city of Memphis. It was a big responsibility. However, it would not last.

While working at Saqqara, Carter ran into some trouble when a fight broke out between Egyptian workers and a group of French tourists.

After he sided with the workers, Carter had trouble finding work on new sites. With his career as an archaeologist seemingly over, Carter tried to make a living selling paintings to tourists. Then in 1906, everything changed.

Carter was asked if he would like to meet English aristocrat George Herbert, better known as Lord Carnarvon. Carnarvon was in Egypt after nearly dying in one of the first ever car accidents in Germany three years earlier. Carnarvon's doctor said he needed to spend his winters in a dry climate, such as Egypt. Carnarvon was a wealthy man who liked spending money on cars and gambling. He was also interested in life after death.

At his three-hundred-room English mansion called Highclere Castle, Carnarvon would invite guests to hold séances. A séance (say: SAY-onz) is a way of trying to talk to the dead. Early twentieth-century séances would take place around a table and were led by a psychic, a person claiming to have special, sometimes inexplicable, powers. Members of the séance would ask questions of their dead relatives, and the psychic would deliver the answers. Some answers would come as knocks on the table—one knock for "yes," and twice for "no." Lord Carnarvon even had his own personal psychic named Velma, who believed that Egyptian pharaohs could put curses on those who disturbed their tombs. Many others believed this, too.

In 1904, English journalist Bertram Fletcher Robinson had written about a pharaoh's curse in England's *Daily Express* newspaper. Robinson said the curse had been brought back from Egypt with a pharaoh's wooden coffin lid called "the Unlucky Mummy." The flat painted board was said to bring misfortune to any involved with it. Robinson wrote: "It is certain that the Egyptians had powers which we in the twentieth century may laugh at, yet can never understand." In 1907, only three years later, Robinson died from a fever. His friends said he had been cursed by the Unlucky Mummy.

Life after death, mummy curses, and pharaohs who held power from beyond the grave were all subjects that Carnarvon loved. He thought digging for Egyptian tombs was a bit like gambling. Nobody knew if they would find anything, but it was worth a shot. Now all Carnarvon needed was an experienced archaeologist to guide him. And Howard Carter was the right person for the job.

# The Unlucky Mummy

The Unlucky Mummy is not a mummy at all. It is a pharaoh's coffin lid, also known as a "mummy board," brought to England from Thebes. And it is believed to be cursed.

The Unlucky Mummy in the British Museum

Stories say two of the four English students who brought the board back from Egypt were injured mysteriously in shooting accidents soon afterward. The other two died in poverty within a short time. A psychic named Madame Helena Blavatsky said the board was evil and suggested it be destroyed. It was given to the British Museum in London, England, where it is still on display today. No one has reported being cursed by the board in recent years.

# CHAPTER 4
## Finding the Pharaoh

Carnarvon and Carter liked each other immediately. Carnarvon had money and wanted to find a tomb, and Carter knew where to look. Carnarvon would sit in the shade of a tent, sipping cool drinks, and watch as Carter directed the Egyptian workers.

Carnarvon had a permit called a concession

to dig near Luxor. The concession meant that Carnarvon had to declare anything he found to the Egyptian Antiquities Service. He could then keep half of the find, while half would stay in Egypt to be exhibited at the Egyptian Museum in Cairo. Carnarvon and Carter were soon sending artifacts to the museum.

After beginning work in 1909, Carter found three tombs containing a total of sixty-four coffins. Alongside the tombs were a few objects not yet taken by tomb robbers, including ivory pieces for a board game called hounds and jackals.

Hounds and jackals

# The Cat Mummy

In 1909, Lord Carnarvon found a small coffin containing a mummified cat. Carnarvon gave the cat to Arthur Weigall, who was inspector general of antiquities in Egypt at the time.

Weigall stored the cat in his home, but then strange things began happening. Weigall's butler was bitten by a scorpion. And he began seeing the ghost of a gray cat. Weigall himself said that the cat mummy turned its head to look at him, with an angry expression on its face. The mummy was put back into its coffin, but it burst open when no one was around.

Had the mummified cat put a curse on Weigall? He was sure it had.

As agreed, Carnarvon sent half of the coffins to the Egyptian Museum. He sold the other half, which were bought by museums around the world.

Although these early finds were notable, Carter and Carnarvon wanted to find an intact pharaoh's tomb that had not been disturbed by robbers. Soon they got their chance. A new concession became available to dig in the Valley of the Kings. Carnarvon snapped it up quickly. Many archaeologists had tried and failed to find new tombs there. They said all the tombs had been discovered. But Carter disagreed. There had been many floods since the tombs were built. The flood water carried large amounts of soil and sand that had covered parts of the valley. Carter believed that there were tombs hidden under this rubble.

Carter had the tomb of a particular pharaoh in mind. Tutankhamun was a minor king who few people knew much about. But while digging in the valley, Carter had discovered a small piece of pottery with Tutankhamun's name on it. This

seemed proof that the pharaoh's tomb was nearby. But Carter searched and searched and could not find it. Years passed. While Carter was sure he would find Tutankhamun's tomb, Carnarvon had doubts. He wasn't interested in funding these digs forever.

In summer 1922, Carnarvon invited Carter to visit him at Highclere Castle. Carter had been to Highclere in 1919, and even attended one of Carnarvon's séances. During the séance, a guest named Helen Cunliffe-Owen started talking in a language that nobody recognized. Nobody, that is, except Howard Carter. He knew the language to be Coptic—the spoken language of ancient Egypt. This event could not be explained.

Now back at Highclere, Carter feared bad news. Sure enough, in front of a roaring fire in a great hall, Carnarvon said he would not pay for another dig. Carter pleaded with Carnarvon for one more try. There was a place in the Valley of the Kings that had not been checked. If the tomb was not there, then he would give up, too.

When Carnarvon heard Carter's pleas, he agreed to one final dig. Carnarvon's change of heart was one of the most important decisions in Egyptian archaeology.

Carter rushed back to the Valley of the Kings. He told his workers to dig below the tomb of the pharaoh Ramses VI. To entertain the workers, Carter brought a caged canary that sang throughout the day. The men thought the bird was a good omen. Before long, they had cleared enough rubble to reveal what Carter had been looking for—twelve steps leading down to a door. Carter immediately sent a telegram to Carnarvon in England: "Have made wonderful discovery in Valley; a magnificent tomb with seals intact."

Now Carter had to wait until Carnarvon arrived in Egypt before proceeding further.

As soon as Carnarvon received Carter's telegram he told his butler to pack his things. The journey by car, train, and ship would take three weeks. Before Carnarvon left, however, he received a warning from a psychic. The man, named Cheiro, said that he had seen a vision of a woman who told him:

"Lord Carnarvon not to enter tomb. Disobey at peril. If ignored would suffer sickness; not recover; death would claim him in Egypt."

Worried, Carnarvon decided to consult his own psychic. Velma said her crystal ball had shown Carnarvon coming out of a tomb, as a hurricane and lightning flashed around him. Velma agreed that Carnarvon was at "great peril" if he traveled to Egypt. But Carnarvon did so anyway.

Carnarvon arrived in the Valley of the Kings on November 22, 1922, with his daughter Evelyn. They ordered the sealed door that Carter had found be removed. Before them was now a thirty-foot passage leading to the tomb. But it was filled with stone rubble that took more time to clear. At the end stood yet another door. On it was stamped Tutankhamun's name. They had found the pharaoh! Carter made an opening in the top corner of the door and used a candle to look in. Then he saw the shapes piled up inside—the "wonderful things"—as he told Carnarvon. But the objects did not look orderly. Had robbers already found the tomb?

They would have to return and investigate later using electric lights. But when he returned to his home, Carter received some distressing news. A cobra had slithered into the house and eaten his canary in its cage. Carter realized the canary must have died around the same time he was breaking into the tomb. He then remembered one of the first things he saw in the flickering candlelight. It was a statue of Tutankhamun wearing the crown of Egypt. On the crown was a uraeus: the cobra rearing up to strike. It was a bad omen; an unwelcome sign of future bad luck.

King Tut's crown

# CHAPTER 5
# Excavating the Tomb

Tutankhamun's tomb was beyond Carter's wildest expectations. It was made up of four rooms that Carter named: the antechamber, annex, burial chamber, and treasury.

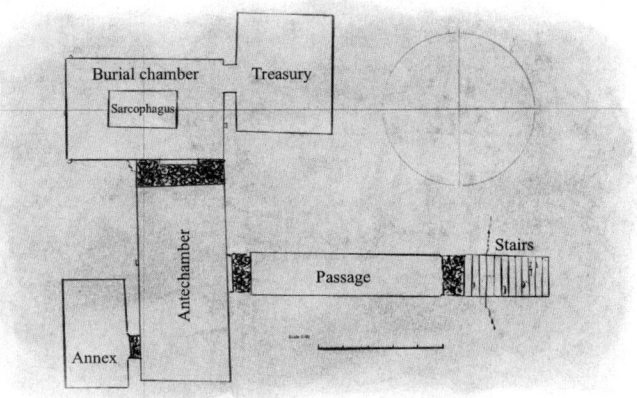

Each room was filled with precious artifacts, but many were in a jumble. Ancient tomb robbers most likely had opened the tomb thousands of years earlier. There was evidence that the main door had been resealed at one point. But any thieves who did enter had left the objects behind.

These objects included hunting weapons, game boards, vases, fans, chairs, beds, and boxes containing bread and meat. Lord Carnarvon would be allowed to keep half of these artifacts after first sending them all to the Egyptian Museum for review. Carter painstakingly recorded, labeled, and packed up every item. There were over 5,300 pieces.

He hired a British team that included archaeologist Arthur Mace, photographer Harry Burton, radiologist Archibald Reid, and secretary Richard Bethell to help. There were also over a dozen Egyptian laborers, including foreman Reis Ahmed Gerigar. The Egyptian workers, however, were superstitious. They had seen a hawk flying above the excavation site, which they said was a bad omen. But nothing would stop Carter excavating Tutankhamun's tomb.

On November 29, Egyptian officials, newspaper journalists, and other invited guests gathered at the public grand opening of Tutankhamun's tomb. Although many reporters attended, only those from English newspaper *The Times* were allowed to go into the tomb. This was because *The Times* had paid Carnarvon a lot of money (around $86,000 in today's money) for exclusive access to the tomb. Other newspapers would therefore have to wait to read the *Times* account before reporting on the latest discoveries. Without having seen the tomb objects, many journalists instead wrote that Tutankhamun's tomb was cursed, which was the kind of story that always sold more newspapers.

One such journalist was Arthur Weigall, the former inspector general of antiquities, now working for the English newspaper the *Daily Mail*. Weigall warned that Lord Carnarvon was joking too much at the tomb opening and not taking it seriously enough. "If he goes down in that spirit, I give him six weeks to live," Weigall said. Others agreed. English novelist Marie Corelli wrote that "the most dire punishment follows any rash intruder into a sealed tomb."

In March 1923, Carnarvon became very ill. A mosquito had bitten him on the cheek and he had nicked the bite while shaving. It became infected and caused blood poisoning. Carnarvon died a few days later from fever in his hotel in Cairo.

Two very strange things happened when Lord Carnarvon died. At the exact moment of death, all the lights went out in the city of Cairo. Back in England, Carnarvon's butler reported that at the very same moment, his dog Susie had stood up, howled, and then dropped down dead.

People immediately blamed what they perceived to be Tutankhamun's curse. Author Arthur Conan Doyle told newspapers that "spirits placed on guard by ancient Egyptian priests to protect the tomb of King Tutankhamun may have caused the death of Lord Carnarvon." French psychic Monsieur Lancelin agreed, saying: "Certain curses were uttered against desecraters of Tutankhamun's tomb." (A desecrater is someone who violates something sacred.) The *New York Times* reported "talk of curses laid by the ancient Egyptians . . . on any who dared disturb the sleep of a Pharaoh."

News of the curse of Tutankhamun spread

fast. Museums in Europe were soon being sent mysterious packages in the mail. They contained Egyptian artifacts, including mummies. The previous owners, terrified of a possible curse, wanted to be rid of these artifacts and so had begun sending them to museums. Carter himself dismissed the curse as "tommyrot" (a British word for nonsense). Despite being sad about his friend and sponsor Lord Carnarvon's death, Carter had

to brush the idea of a curse aside and continue excavating the tomb.

This involved Tutankhamun's objects being photographed, wrapped in cotton and cloth, and then put into crates for delivery by boat down the Nile River to Cairo. Outside the tomb, newspaper reporters and members of the public waited and hoped to catch a glimpse of the treasures.

There were gasps as some objects too large for crates were carried to the boat. These included statues of the pharaoh, wooden beds with ivory headrests, and a child-size throne with a picture of Tutankhamun and Ankhesenamun made from pounded gold. In the scene, the queen is touching the arm of the seated king. It is a tender moment recorded for eternity.

Apart from Carter's team, only *The Times* journalists and important guests were allowed into the tomb itself. These guests included famous actors, politicians, members of royal families, and wealthy businesspeople. One such guest was George Jay Gould, an American millionaire.

Gould visited the tomb in May 1923, but then became ill with a fever. He died shortly afterward. Only a month later, Egyptian prince Ali Kamel Fahmy Bey visited the tomb. He was then murdered by his wife. Newspapers were quick to report on these latest victims of "the curse."

Responding to reporters' questions about the existence of a possible curse annoyed Carter. He said: "It is rather too much to ask me to believe that some spook is keeping watch and ward over the dead Pharaoh, ready to wreak vengeance on anyone who goes too near." But this did not satisfy the press.

Stories emerged that a tablet had been found near the tomb entrance containing the following words: "Death will slay with its wings whoever disturbs the peace of the pharaoh." Some said Carter destroyed this tablet before his superstitious Egyptian workers saw it. Another story said a second curse had been found on a tomb statue. This one said: "It is I who drive back robbers of the tomb with flames of the desert. I am the protector of Tutankhamun's grave." Some said Carter had scratched the words off the statue. But nobody knew whether this was true, or just another rumor.

At the end of 1923, there was yet another death. This time it was Lord Carnarvon's half brother, Aubrey Herbert. Herbert had died from blood poisoning caused by dental surgery. Many were convinced the curse was actually to blame.

Aubrey Herbert

As Carter closed up the site of Tutankhamun's tomb for the summer, the public wondered what would happen next. Would there be even more deaths? Would Carter finally find a curse bound up in the pharaoh's wrappings? In 1924, Carter would open Tutankhamun's burial chamber for the world to find out.

# Tut-Mania

The discovery of Tutankhamun's tomb in 1922 sparked a new craze in all things related to ancient Egypt, in Europe and the United States. This was called "Tut-mania." Ancient Egyptian designs were used on clothes, jewelry, and furniture. Fashion models advertised products wearing short cropped "Egyptian" haircuts, snake bracelets, and uraeus (cobra) headbands. Egyptian hieroglyphs, palm trees, and pyramids were pictured on everything from cookie containers, to soap, clocks, and cigar boxes.

That same year, US president Herbert Hoover even named his pet dog "King Tut."

US president Herbert Hoover with dog, King Tut

# CHAPTER 6
## Unwrapping the Mummy

There was great excitement when Carter returned to excavate Tutankhamun's burial chamber, which was the second room of four in the tomb. The burial chamber was perhaps the biggest prize. Some wanted to see the actual mummy, while others wondered if opening the chamber held its own curse.

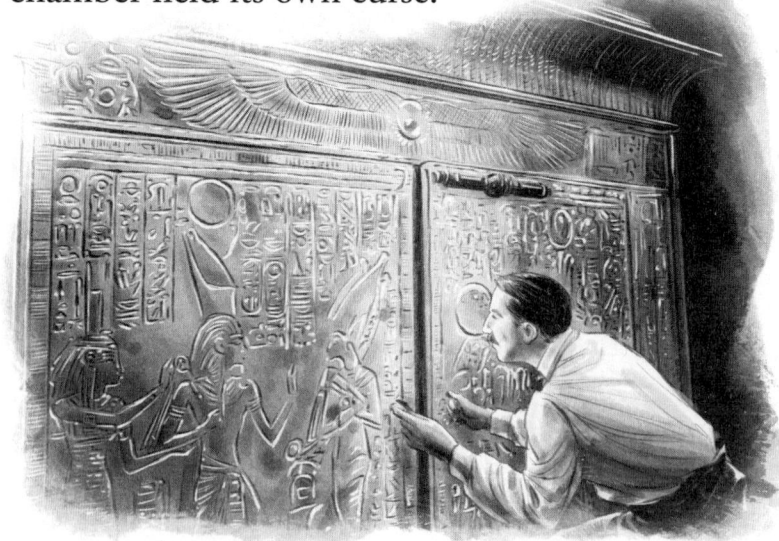

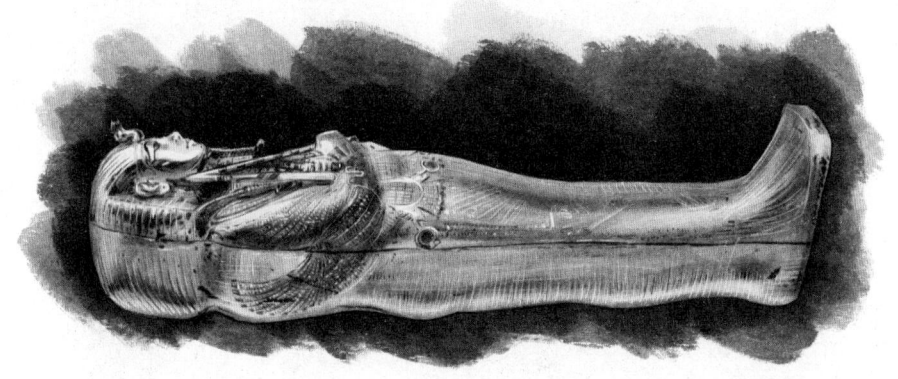

Getting to the mummy was tricky. The small burial chamber was almost completely filled by three giant boxes of pounded gold, one inside the other. These were taken apart to reveal a stone sarcophagus. What would be inside?

On February 12, 1924, Carter held a ceremony inside the burial chamber. Special guests attended to watch the opening of the sarcophagus. The room fell silent as ropes and pulleys slowly lifted the heavy granite lid. Then, with flashlight in hand, Carter looked inside. At first he was disappointed. Dark linen cloth covered everything.

As Carter removed the linen, he revealed a coffin in the image of Tutankhamun. It was wooden and painted gold. This was another amazing discovery for Carter. However, he would go no further that day and the ceremony ended. Then the very next day, trouble began.

While Carter's excavation had been going on, Egypt had gained its independence from Britain. The Egyptian government was now in charge and they wanted things to change. Carter was told that a member of the Antiquities Service would be at the excavation at all times. When Egyptian officials canceled a planned visit to the tomb by the wives of the excavation team, Carter was furious. He locked the iron gate to the tomb and took away the only key. No one was going to tell him who could visit his excavation!

The Egyptian government said Carter had forty-eight hours to return and continue the excavation. But Carter refused. And that was a mistake. The government canceled the concession to dig in the Valley of the Kings, the prize so valued by Carter and Carnarvon. It meant all the objects found in the tomb would now stay in Egypt. Tutankhamun's tomb was then opened to the public, so ordinary Egyptians could see the tomb of one of their own pharaohs.

In January 1924, excavation team member Archibald Reid died during surgery. Had the curse struck again? Then team member Arthur Mace collapsed suddenly. He would remain in poor health until dying of arsenic poisoning four years later. In April 1924, Carter arrived in New York to begin a lecture tour of the United States. He was still hopeful that he could reach an agreement with Egyptian officials and return to the Valley of the Kings. Then on November 20, 1924, Lee Stack, a high-ranking British official, was shot dead by a terrorist in Cairo.

Lee Stack

Tutankhamun's curse was blamed for all these deaths. But the Stack assassination had the greatest effect on the excavation of the tomb.

It meant that the British government temporarily took back control of Egypt. Carter was therefore invited to return and finish his excavation. When he arrived at the site, Tutankhamun's wooden coffin was still there, waiting to be opened. What would be inside?

After taking off the coffin lid, there was a surprise—another coffin lay inside. Like the first, it was covered with gold and decorated with red and blue stones. What was inside this coffin stunned Carter. It was yet another coffin,

but one made of solid gold. This coffin contained the mummified body of Tutankhamun.

One final wonder greeted Carter: a golden mask that covered the mummy's head. But there was more—dozens of objects were tucked into the mummy's linen wrappings. Was one of these a parchment or tablet detailing Tutankhamun's curse? The team readied itself to reveal the pharaoh's body.

But the mummy was covered in a thick resin that kept it stuck to the coffin. This caused Carter to handle the body roughly. The legs, arms, and head were all cut off in an effort to remove the mummy from the coffin. This treatment of their dead pharaoh would have horrified the ancient Egyptians. Those responsible would have been immediately put to death. If the pharaoh's curse was real, Carter's team would surely not be able to escape it now.

So what did they find? Within the bandages,

there were over 150 different precious objects. These included necklaces, collars, and bracelets made of gold. There were amulets in the shape of gods and animals, and a hawk-shaped brooch made of gold.

Each object was put there to protect the pharaoh on his journey to the afterlife. Egyptian priests would have said prayers and spells over the objects to give them special powers. However, there was no sign of a written curse. Finally, to finish the investigation, Tutankhamun's mask had to be removed. The

face of the young king stared back, blankly. His skin looked like dark leather. The empty eyes had been filled with black fabric.

# The Gold Death Mask

Tutankhamun's death mask is considered one of the finest ancient objects ever discovered. Weighing around twenty-four pounds, the mask is made from solid gold and fitted with semiprecious stones, such as lapis lazuli and quartz. It is shaped like a long helmet and shows the face of Tutankhamun wearing the uraeus headdress, ready to spit fire at his enemies.

Today, the mask is regarded as a masterpiece of ancient art and a symbol of Egypt itself. It is on permanent display in the Egyptian Museum in Cairo.

Then Carter noticed something odd. On Tutankhamun's cheek was a small hole, just like the mosquito bite that had killed Carnarvon. Was this a strange and scary coincidence, or evidence of Tutankhamun's curse at work? What would happen now to the men who had just pulled apart the body of the pharaoh? If there was to be a punishment, certainly they would be next.

Georges Benedite

Sure enough, tragedy struck again as Carter continued on during the last years of the excavation. In 1926, French archaeologist Georges Benedite dropped dead outside the tomb. Doctors said he had died of a stroke, a blockage of blood to the brain. Then in 1929, Carter's former secretary Richard Bethell was found dead at his club in London.

The cause of death was probably suffocation. Newspapers were quick to link the death to the pharaoh's curse. "Tut-Ankh-Amen 'Curse' Recalled by Death" a *New York Times* headline read. But then things became even stranger, and more frightening.

Richard Bethell

Only three months after Bethell's death, his father, Lord Westbury, jumped out of a seventh-story window. In a note, Westbury said "I really cannot stand any more horrors." Some newspapers reported

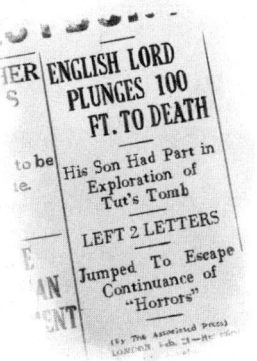

that Westbury had been muttering about "the curse of the pharaohs" before he died. Australian newspaper *The Mail* reported Westbury's death on the front page with the headline "Fourteenth Victim of Tutankhamun's Curse." The newspaper also said Egypt scholar J. C. Mardrus had found a curse warning intruders against entering Tutankhamun's tomb, or otherwise: "The royal Uraeus who lords it on my brow shall belch forth fire against their heads." Mardrus could not produce any evidence. But the Westbury death took another twist during the funeral, when the car carrying Lord Westbury's body slid off the road and killed an eight-year-old boy.

Carter himself finally finished his excavation of Tutankhamun's tomb in 1932. He was still in good health. If the curse was real, then why was Carter still alive? His last act at the tomb was to put back together Tutankhamun's skeleton and return it to its sarcophagus. It is the only object left in the tomb for tourists to see today. Carter then retired at his home in London.

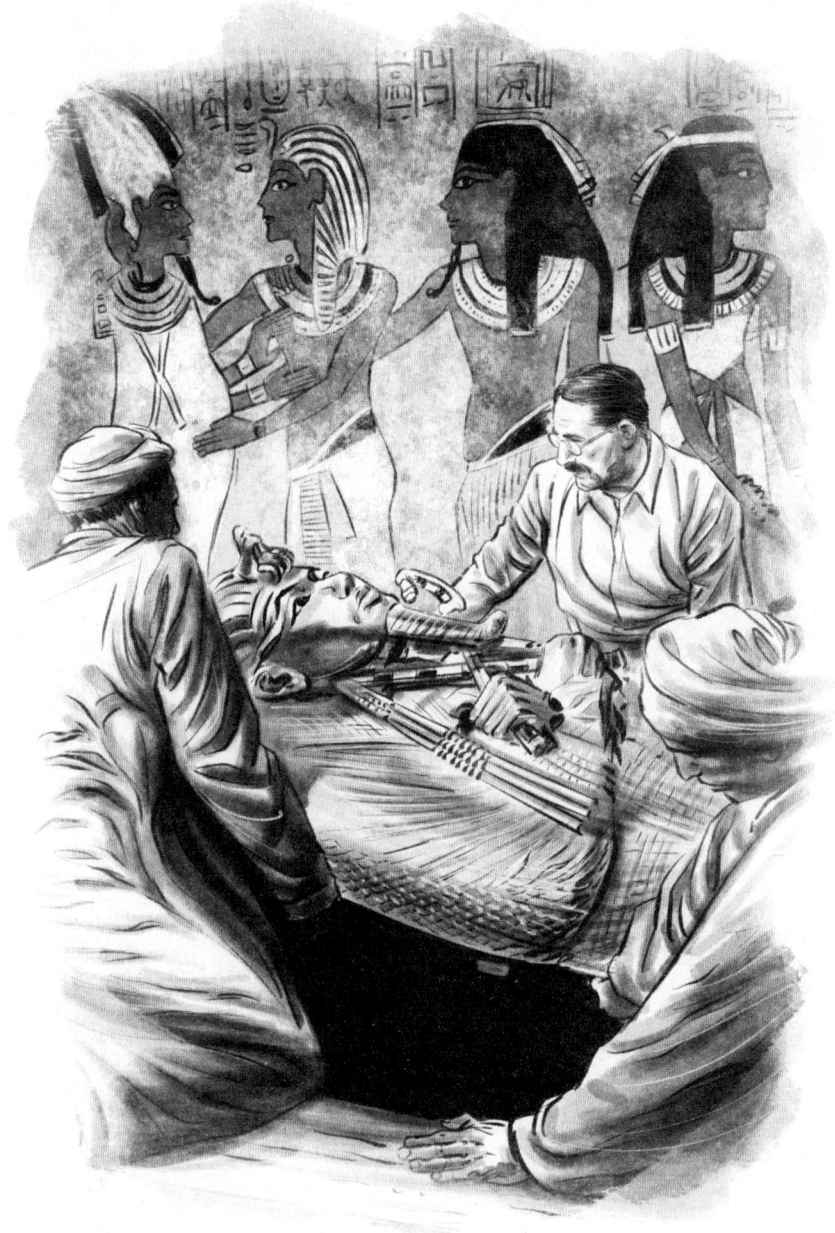

# Movie Mummy

The legend of Tutankhamun's curse was kept alive by the 1932 American movie *The Mummy*. The movie features an ancient mummy that comes back to life to look for his lost wife, with terrible consequences. Starring famous horror actor Boris

Karloff, *The Mummy* is considered a classic that sparked many other mummy movies. These include *The Mummy's Hand* (1940), *The Curse of the Mummy's Tomb* (1964), and *The Curse of King Tut's Tomb* (1980).

More recently, a 1999 movie called *The Mummy* was a blockbuster hit that led to several sequels and 2017's *The Mummy*, starring Tom Cruise.

In the end, Carter did not die from Tutankhamun's curse, but the work of excavating the tomb for a decade had exhausted him. He turned away from public life and then became ill with cancer. He died in 1939, at sixty-four years old.

# CHAPTER 7
# The Eternal Curse

In the years after Carter's death, Tut-mania eventually faded. The story of Tutankhamun's curse stayed quiet for many decades. Then in the 1960s, several museum tours of Tutankhamun's treasures were organized. Between 1962 and

1981, the artifacts would be flown around the world and displayed in Europe, Japan, Canada, and the United States. And strange things began happening to people involved with the exhibits.

In 1972, Egyptian director of antiquities Gamal Mehrez was organizing an overseas tour of Tutankhamun's treasures. But as the treasures were being packaged up, Mehrez had a heart attack and died. The flight crew of the plane that was shipping the treasures also suffered misfortune. One member of the crew broke their leg on the crate containing Tutankhamun's death mask,

and another came home to find their house burned to the ground. Two other members of the flight crew died in mysterious circumstances only a few years later.

Another mysterious event took place at the opening of the 1972 Tutankhamun exhibition at the British Museum. One of the guests was Evelyn Herbert, Lord Carnarvon's daughter. Now seventy years old, Herbert told reporters at the opening that she did not believe in Tutankhamun's curse.

However, after leaving the museum, Herbert fell down and suffered a stroke that left her paralyzed. She was in poor health for the remaining eight years of her life.

Was Tutankhamun's curse to blame for all this misfortune—or was it simply coincidence? In 2002, Australian scientist Mark Nelson set out to try to solve the mystery. To do this, he looked at the twenty-five people most closely involved with the excavation of Tutankhamun's tomb. These

Mark Nelson

were the people who had been at the tomb opening, excavated the artifacts, or helped unwrap Tutankhamun's mummy. Nelson reasoned that this group would have been most likely to have been affected by a curse. But instead of dying under mysterious circumstances, Nelson found most had lived to around seventy and had simply died of old age. Publishing his results in the *British Medical Journal*, Nelson said there was no evidence of a curse.

The story of the curse, however, persisted. In 2005, Egypt's minister of antiquities, Zahi Hawass, conducted a computed tomography (CT) scan of Tutankhamun's skeleton. A CT scan is like a 3D X-ray. Hawass hoped it would shed light on how the pharaoh died. Interestingly, the scan showed Tutankhamun had not died from a blow to the head, as some suspected. However, Hawass said odd things happened during the time of the scan:

"I cannot dismiss the legend of the curse because today many things happened. We almost had an accident in a car, the wind blew up in the Valley of the Kings, and the computer of the CT scan was completely stopped for two hours,"

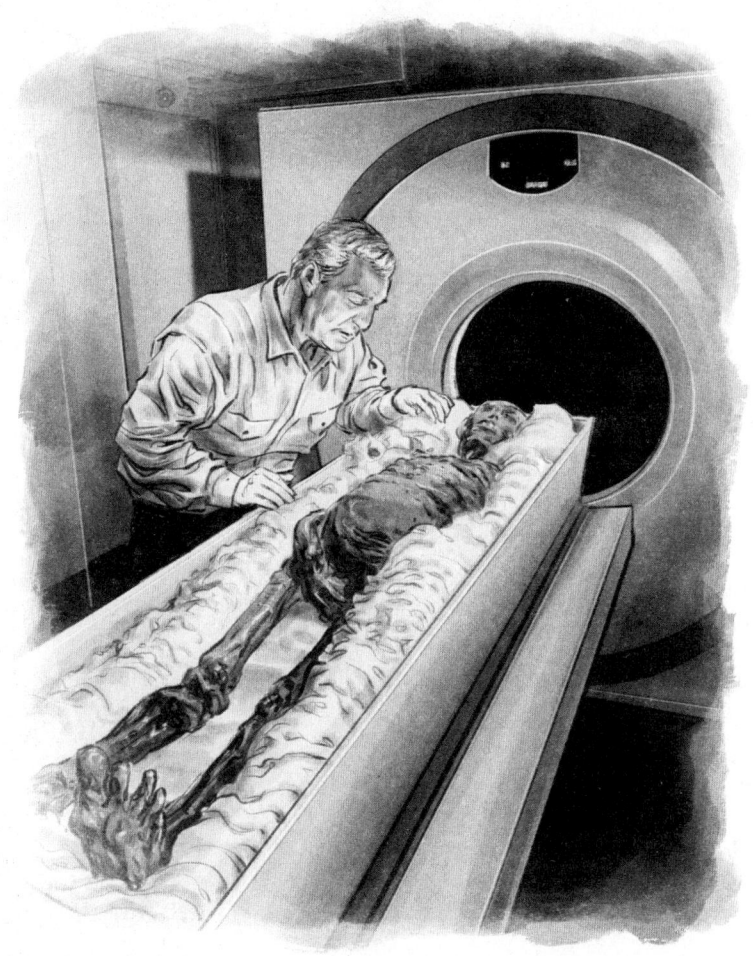

Hawass said.

The CT scan could not prove evidence of a curse, but could science help in other ways?

Perhaps the curse was not a supernatural spell

Dr. Nicola Di Paolo

from beyond the grave but bacteria released when the tomb was opened? This could have infected the lungs of people entering the tomb, even after thousands of years. Italian doctor Nicola Di Paolo and German microbiologist Gotthard Kramer said mold in the tomb could carry such harmful bacteria.

Laboratory studies were carried out on Egyptian mummies and found they contained *Aspergillus* (say: AS-per-gi-luhs) mold, which can cause bleeding in the lungs. The dangerous bacteria *Pseudomonas* (say: SOO-duh-mow-nuhs) and *Staphylococcus* (say: STA-fuh-luh-kaa-kuhs) were also found on the walls of Tutankhamun's tomb. Was the case of the curse finally solved?

A 2013 Harvard University study said no. University scientists studied the possibility of bacteria, including in brown spots on the walls of Tutankhamun's tomb. They did find bacteria there, but ruled that it was no longer active and so would pose no threat to visitors.

However, more than one hundred years since the discovery of Tutankhamun's tomb, stories about his curse continue. This is partly because of the lasting impact of newspaper reports from the time of the tomb's discovery. But it is also due to the mystery and wonder of ancient Egypt itself. When the pharaoh's tomb was opened in 1922, people marveled at Egyptian preparations for a life after death. Everything Tutankhamun needed for eternity was buried with him. Perhaps, therefore, the ancient Egyptians held a special secret about life after death that had been forgotten in modern times? If this were true, it was not difficult to imagine the Egyptians also had special powers for creating curses. And if anyone deserved to be cursed, surely it was a robber who disturbed a pharaoh's final resting place. Maybe Tutankhamun himself even had some supernatural power to punish people from beyond the grave.

Tutankhamun is considered to be a minor

king. Few people had even heard of him when Carter began searching for his tomb. The pharaoh ruled for only ten years and did not live to reach adulthood. He died mysteriously and his tomb was prepared in haste. And yet, in 2022, thousands of people gathered in Luxor to celebrate the one-hundred-year anniversary of the discovery of Tutankhamun's tomb.

Howard Carter's house in Luxor

The anniversary events included a virtual tour in the Valley of the Kings, the reopening of Howard Carter's restored house, and a conference featuring speeches by George and Fiona Carnarvon, the descendants of Lord Carnarvon. There was even an opera about Tutankhamun's life written by Zahi Hawass.

This is the legacy left by Tutankhamun and Howard Carter. Over three thousand years since his death, Tutankhamun is remembered as Egypt's most famous pharaoh. Millions of people around the world know his name. In this way, Tutankhamun—ancient Egypt's boy king—lives on for eternity. But forever tied to Tutankhamun is the idea of a possible curse: an ancient punishment for those who disturb the pharaoh's rest. Perhaps we will never be sure if it is real or not.

# Stolen Artifacts

In 2022, letters were discovered that show Howard Carter had stolen small Tutankhamun treasures and given them away. Carter offered one such gift—an amulet taken from the pharaoh's body—to British scholar Alan Gardiner in 1934. The letters came to light at a time when Egypt has increased calls for its ancient artifacts to be returned from foreign museums.

In 2010, New York's Metropolitan Museum of Art returned nineteen objects taken from Tutankhamun's tomb. These included a tiny bronze dog and part of a bracelet. More museums followed this example. In 2021, over 5,300 ancient Egyptian artifacts from around the world were returned to Egypt. These can now be seen in the Egyptian Museum, alongside the treasures from Tutankhamun's tomb.

# Timeline of the Curse
# of King Tut's Tomb

| | |
|---|---|
| **1323 BCE** | Pharaoh Tutankhamun dies suddenly at eighteen years old and is buried in the Valley of the Kings |
| **1798 CE** | French general Napoleon Bonaparte invades Egypt |
| **1817** | Italian Giovanni Belzoni begins stealing precious ancient artifacts from Egypt |
| **1827** | English author Jane C. Loudon publishes *The Mummy!*, a novel about an Egyptian pharaoh coming back to life |
| **1891** | Seventeen-year-old Englishman Howard Carter travels to Egypt to draw ancient artifacts |
| **1906** | Howard Carter is introduced to Lord Carnarvon. The pair join forces to search for an intact pharaoh's tomb |
| **1922** | Howard Carter discovers Tutankhamun's tomb containing "wonderful things" on November 26 |
| **1923** | Lord Carnarvon dies from an infected mosquito bite on April 5. Newspapers blame "Tutankhamun's Curse" |
| **1924** | Tutankhamun's tomb is opened to ordinary Egyptians after Howard Carter is locked out in March |
| **1929** | Carter's former secretary Richard Bethell is found dead. Bethell's father kills himself three months later |
| **1932** | Movie *The Mummy* starring Boris Karloff is released |
| **2022** | The one hundredth anniversary of the opening of Tutankhamun's tomb is celebrated in Luxor, Egypt |

# Timeline of the World

1330 BCE — Mursilis II becomes king of the Hittite Empire, in modern-day Turkey and beyond

1798 CE — The United States Navy is established by President John Adams

1815 — French emperor Napoleon is defeated by the armies of Britain, Prussia, and the Netherlands at the Battle of Waterloo

1906 — The San Francisco earthquake destroys most of the city and leaves over three thousand people dead

1922 — The Irish Free State is established after the war of independence with Britain

1923 — Nazi Party leader Adolf Hitler is arrested for staging an uprising against the German government in Munich

1924 — Athletes from forty-four countries compete in the Summer Olympics in Paris, France

1929 — The stock market crashes in Wall Street, New York, leading to the worldwide Great Depression

1932 — The Sydney Harbour Bridge opens in Sydney, Australia

2013 — Barack Obama is sworn in for a second term as president of the United States

2022 — The number of COVID-19 vaccines given worldwide reaches ten billion

# Bibliography

*Books for young readers

Brier, Bob. *Tutankhamun and the Tomb that Changed the World*. Oxford: Oxford University Press, 2022.

Carter, Howard, and A. C. Mace. *The Tomb of Tutankhamun: Volume 1*. London: Bloomsbury, 2014.

*Edwards, Roberta. *Who Was King Tut?* New York: Penguin Workshop, 2006.

*Fleming, Candace. *The Curse of the Mummy: Uncovering Tutankhamun's Tomb*. New York: Scholastic, 2021.

Frayling, Christopher. *The Face of Tutankhamun*. London: Faber & Faber, 1992.

*Green, Jen. *Tutankhamen's Tomb*. New York: Barron's Juveniles, 2006.

*Keenan, Sheila. *What Is the Story of the Mummy?* New York: Penguin Workshop, 2021.

Luckhurst, Roger. *The Mummy's Curse: The True History of a Dark Fantasy*. Oxford: Oxford University Press, 2012.

Reeves, Nicholas. *The Complete Tutankhamun*. London: Thames and Hudson, 1990.

Tyldesley, Joyce. *Tutankhamen: The Search for an Egyptian King*. New York: Basic Books, 2012.